Enlightened Wealth

A Manual for Beginning Your Personal MoneyMinding® Journey

Tracy Piercy, CFP

250-592-0457 or 1-877-764-6444
www.MoneyMinding.com
info@MoneyMinding.com

ISBN 0-9780616-3-2

Cover photo by Frances Litman, www.FrancesLitman.com
Book layout by Kelly Hewkin, www.IntuitiveGraphicDesign.com

First edition published by MoneyMinding® Inc. 2006
Enlightened Wealth Journal Published by
MoneyMinding® Inc. 2006

Printed in Canada

_____

Gifted To

_____

With Blessings From

_____

Date

~ *Believe ~ Begin ~ Become* ~

Dedication

To Joe,
My wonderful husband who really knows the
'believe, begin, become' in our lives!!

ENLIGHTENED WEALTH

Table of Contents

Preface

While this book is about personal finances, there is no intention to provide financial planning advice. Neither the publisher nor the author is engaged in rendering professional advice or services to the individual reader. The ideas, procedures and suggestions contained in this book are not intended as a substitute for consulting with your financial advisor. They should, however, complement that relationship. The material presented here is entirely for information, inspiration and encouragement. Neither the author nor the publisher nor MoneyMinding Inc. shall be liable or responsible for any loss or damage allegedly arising from any information or suggestion in this book.

Wherever quotations are made, all precaution has been taken to give credit to the original author. However, sometimes a similar quotation can come from several sources. The author apologizes for any such discrepancies.

Acknowledgements

This manual exists because of a few special people. You
likely already know who you are, but your incredible support,
encouragement and friendship need extra special thanks!!

Of course, my husband, Joe: what a journey we're sharing. Where
would I be without you? Thank you. I love you. You are more than
I ever asked for, and I am grateful for you in my life every day!
I never seem to know how to thank you enough, but none of this
would be happening without you.

And my beautiful daughter, Jordyn, who is the real inspiration
behind the daily questions: you have been answering them since
you could barely talk. Thank you for all that you are and for all that
you bring into my/our life.

Gail Watson, oh how much your friendship has meant to me.
Thank you for all that you are – to me and to so many others.

Kerry Brown, you always seem to know just what to say.

Dave and Sara Mansi, you have always been supportive and I always love the times we share. Thank you for encouraging me to write this manual.

Sue Ranzinger, look how far we've come and I still feel like we're just beginning.

Jim Jacobson, thank you always for sharing your vision, your knowledge and your encouragement.

Kelly Hewkin, thank you for your enthusiasm, flexibility and ongoing belief.

Thank you, as well, to all the mentors, authors, speakers and inspiring leaders who have been my friends and supporters through your published works. You never know who or how you'll touch someone's life, but I could always count on just the right words from a trusted friend (and author) when I needed them most. Tony Robbins, you got me started; Les Brown, you picked me up; Mark Victor Hansen, you got me moving; and everyone else, you kept me, and keep me going.

And certainly not last: thank you to my heavenly Father and my real Daddy. You have always loved me even when I didn't feel that lovable! And Mom, if you were still here… I love you and miss you always. Thank you!

Tracy Piercy
Spring 2006

BELIEVE

Welcome

Let me tell you how this book came to be and why I can confidently say it will change your life. It has changed mine, and the lives of many others who have used the material, long before there was even an idea of a book.

Enlightened Wealth is about writing your story—or, in some cases, rewriting your story. It is the first step in your journey to becoming all you can be without financial limitations; without financial stress; without guilt, fear, judgment or frustration around money. This is about your journey, like mine. Others before you have said, "We want and deserve more. We don't know how, but we believe enough to know that if someone else has done something similar, we can too."

Late in 2001, after a fight lasting several years, my husband and I finally lost a financial battle when we weren't strong enough financially to continue to fight a tax audit. It seemed that, for as long as I could remember, we had been burdened with some sort of financial pressure, even though we earned more than I ever

imagined at the time. The two years leading up to our financial collapse were a pressure cooker series of one step forward, then slam—another problem. When we eventually surrendered, we didn't have the resources to pay the amount the government wanted or to continue to fight for what we believed. For a financial advisor teaching about success principles, being cornered into bankruptcy was devastating.

While still reeling from this money loss, two months later, early in 2002, my mother died suddenly. She was only 59. This was also the first time I remember hearing my father cry—really cry. A month later, my father-in-law was diagnosed with cancer while holidaying, and I thought my mother-in-law was going to die from stress as she fought to drive the two of them back into the country safely for medical treatment. My brother and his children struggled to survive a devastating marriage breakup, and then my father's mother (my grandmother) died a few months after that. Within a couple of years, my father had met and married a wonderful lady. My other brother was marrying, my uncle (my mom's brother) was battling cancer and my other grandmother (my mother's mom) died too.

Family, friends, health, relationships: funny how the money issues seemed less important now.

My husband and I had a wake-up call. Prior to this, we had lived pretty average, middle-class lifestyles—meaning, basically, that nothing dramatic or unusual happened. Our families were all together, we were all healthy and had careers and families, we all owned homes, blah, blah, blah…

This might not be your story, but your story is about what resonates today in your own life because of your life experiences and

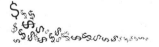

choices. Designing your life is about what you do with your stories to make them unique and wonderful life experiences. How do you learn to see through your story to make something significant, something where others may benefit from your experiences and/or something that is about more than just money?

We have so much to be grateful for, so much to live for, so much to enjoy and only so much time! What are you waiting for—a wake-up call? Or do you think your time has run out because you've already reached a certain age and it's too late to pursue your dreams? Could I have written this book, started my company and done all the things I am doing now without the tools you are about to discover? I'm going to say, "Absolutely not!" I was too caught up in the circumstances as they were. The gap between where I thought I "should" be, where I wanted to be and where I currently was, was far, far too big—and getting bigger.

Your journey begins here. I will help you write your story the way you want it, help you become the person of your dreams and help you put the pieces together financially so it's not about the money. Rather, it's about your family, friends, health, relationships and other causes that are important to you. The money "how-to" strategies are necessary, and they will come, but after you know why and what for.

Your journey begins here first and always comes back to here. This is a part of the financial plan that doesn't ever go away. It will grow with you and guide you as your life unfolds. Without this foundation, there will always be the tendency to look at the difference between what was, what could have been, what should be and what isn't. You make your money decisions and establish the money strategies that reflect who you are, where you're going, what you want and what you believe.

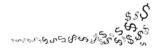

Start now and begin the process. It's not about the money; it's about what the money can do for you and for others.

~ *Believe* ~ *Begin* ~ *Become* ~

Introduction

Enlightened means: "1: highly educated; having extensive information or understanding; 2: having knowledge and spiritual insight; 3: freed from illusion; 4: having or based on relevant experience" (WordNet ® 2.0, © 2003, Princeton University).

Wealth means: "1: the state of being rich and affluent; having a plentiful supply of material goods and money; 2: the quality of profuse abundance; 3: an abundance of material possessions and resources; 4: property that has economic utility; 5: a monetary value or an exchange value" (WordNet ® 2.0, © 2003, Princeton University).

MoneyMinding® is the process of implementing the principles of enlightenment into the management and creation of wealth. This book is designed primarily to support you in the "enlightened" part of "enlightened wealth."

If it's personal financial independence you're looking for, this is where you start and where you return to throughout the wealth

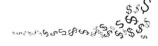

9

creation and management process. This enlightened part of wealth is the key to change, key to growth, key to success, and key to success with money.

Enlightenment is the integral part of wealth creation and management that guides how we think. We might know we need to change some behavior or that a particular course of action would be good for us, but until we believe it, we aren't likely to do anything about it. My husband likes to use the phrase, "To know and not to do is not to know." There are many examples in life outside of financial areas that we can use to illustrate the significance of this: exercising, quitting smoking, eating healthier, etc.

In finance, if you want to get different results than you have in the past, you have to learn to think differently. Maybe you will need to learn how to read different books, how to talk to different people, how to change your spending habits or how to invest some time in learning and understanding financial matters. You will know what needs to be addressed as you implement other MoneyMinding® steps and strategies outlined in the diagram at the back of your Enlightened Wealth book.

Change is uncomfortable—even if it's for the better. In Enlightened Wealth, you will have a place to get clear on what's really important to you and where you really want to go. The "Daily Review" section of your journey is designed to help you see what's happening throughout the day that is inspiring you, supporting your vision or things that could be improved. It's a tool to help you become accountable to your goals and to develop greater clarity about your true priorities.

While this book refers to 12 groups, each with 31 sets of review questions, you will likely not complete an entire year before moving on. You will either already know what area of your personal finances needs to be addressed or you will be working with someone who is helping you move forward. Either way, when you are approaching something new or different, or when you want to make a positive change, or are uncomfortable addressing the gap that exists between where you'd like to be and where you are, this is the support you'll find in Enlightened Wealth. It is your support, your accountability, your priorities and your vision all wrapped into one incredibly powerful, unique, enlightened wealth-building tool.

Give

We are always giving. Sometimes we're not aware of what we're giving: friendship, companionship, a friendly smile, financial support, gifts, support for causes we believe in, our time, charitable donations.

Learning to give, as well as to receive, is a component of MoneyMinding®. As such, you will find that part of your journey will be about helping you recognize the giving you already do. It will be about helping you realize all the wonderful things you already do have in your life. It will also be about helping you realize all the possibilities you have to experience and share throughout your journey.

One of the sharing and giving choices I have made is to contribute 10 percent of all the proceeds from this book to charity. The MoneyMinding® Foundation supports empowering children's initiatives. One of the organizations it sponsors is Watoto, a charity whose mission is to raise future leaders from the millions of orphaned children in Uganda.

Your journey will touch many people's lives, from your immediate families to strangers across the ocean. Share what you can and watch the miracles unfold, not only in your life, but also all around you.

Best Wishes to You!

You are on a journey. Whatever your current situation, whatever your goals, you can be, do and have whatever your heart desires. How do I know? Because you're reading this right now and that tells me you already have an interest in making things bigger and better than they are today in your own life or for others. That's all it takes.

What is "enlightened wealth"? What is "MoneyMinding®"? They are the process of implementing into daily practice the proven, universal success principles and practical financial planning strategies. The objective is to create individual financial peace and independence where money is not an obstacle or stressor in your life, where money is the catalyst for enjoyment, fulfillment and significance in the lives of others.

Because money means different things to different people, one of the first MoneyMinding® steps is to become aware of your own lifestyle desires so you can structure your financial life to support that desired lifestyle. From there, you implement structures,

strategies and a foundation that will build and support that lifestyle. Ultimately, this is financial independence: freedom from financial stress, freedom to be you, freedom to do what you really want with your life, for yourself and for others. You become "enlightened wealthy," not just "money wealthy."

The process begins first with gratitude for where you are now and with an awareness of your desires. The gap between where you are and where you want to be is the "yawning chasm" that often stops people from looking beyond their current situation to what can be. We get comfortable with our own situation (even if it's not really that comfortable) and keep looking to make changes only from within our own reality. You need to get past your current situation and take your eyes off yourself to be able to see what can be, rather than simply what is.

As your vision for your future becomes clearer and you realize that exactly where you are today is a wonderful place to be, you become more enlightened about the possibilities for your future and for others. You will find that you will become more aware of opportunities that will help you move closer to the ideal vision.

There is a wonderful saying: "Watch your thoughts; they become words. Watch your words; they become actions. Watch your actions; they become habits. Watch your habits; they become character. Watch your character; it becomes your destiny." This is how it starts—and builds—and continues.

Your Enlightened Wealth book is a tool, a program and a guide to help you begin to implement success principles or to stay on track with your current program. This program is interactive, hands-on learning that is insightful and is the foundational process within the complete MoneyMinding® program.

This book will help you develop vision, set and achieve personal goals and gain valuable insight into your highest life priorities. It is part of your journey. It's where you write your story, get focused, stay focused and learn that if you can think about possibilities while building the financial structure to support and encourage them, they will become reality. Your thinking determines the decisions you make, which ultimately determine your destiny and the legacy you leave behind.

Awareness is vital to your enjoyment of life and to fulfilling your life's purpose. What do you really wish for? Why? What will it mean to your life if this is present today? What will it mean to your life if this is never present? These are the questions you will ask and find answers to, along your journey.

"Wouldn't that be nice." "Oh, I wish." "They got lucky." Oh, the misery of comparison! The sighs of settling for what is rather than being grateful for what can be! You can choose to curse the person who has what you want or to condemn yourself for not having it. Or, you can choose to bless those who already have something that appeals to your heart, your values and your longing.

When you are attracted to something or someone and they appeal to who you are or would like to become, you can do one of two things. You can wish that the thing, person or event was in your life or you can set out to create that thing, event, or feeling to become more like the person who appealed to you.

There are different levels of wishing. There is the wish you make when you throw a penny into a fountain or blow out the candles on a birthday cake. There is the wish you make when you see something you like. And there is the wish you make when you compare yourself and your situation to someone else.

The first kind of wishing is fun. For a brief moment, you fantasize about what might be. This is not unlike the fantasy you experience if you imagine winning the lottery. It can be fun to imagine the results. It can also become a valuable tool to visualize what your life could be like.

If you become aware of your fantasies, you can gain insight as to how you might like to live your life and what qualities in the fantasy appeal to you. Then you can learn how to make that fantasy a reality and how to bring its qualities into your own life—unless, of course, the fantasy stays buried under the consciousness of your current reality and is squashed by the second kind of wishful thinking: the unfulfilled wish-list.

If you considered the things that might go on a Christmas wish list, the reason they are there is that you feel they would give you pleasure. Interestingly, the items that would go on a gift wish list are usually items that you perceive you might have a chance of receiving. In other words, you evaluate your true desires before you even put the items on the list. This means that if something makes it to the list, you have an expectation and a hope that these things might actually become reality in your life. If you don't put them on the list, they might still be desires, but you abandon any hope and close your mind to the possibility that they might become part of your reality some day in the future.

What happens to the items that didn't make the list or that made the list but didn't get received? Do you continue to wish for them? Do you let them go? Do you feel disappointed? How do you respond to not receiving these wishes? That is the key to whether they create voids somewhere in your life or resentment or nothing at all. To understand wishes is to recognize that there is a desire for

something so that the wish is conscious and can then be dealt with on a conscious level.

When wishes make it to a written list, they at least have the potential of being realized, just like goals. When they aren't written down, with a date on them, they are just fantasies. When wishes remain in your head and aren't shared and written, they will always remain fantasies. They will always consume mental energy and will have almost no chance of becoming reality. These kinds of wishes will, however, have the possibility of influencing the third type of wish: comparisons.

Comparison wishing creates an uncertainty and a lack of confidence and self-esteem. Suddenly, the other person or other thing is more valuable than what you currently have in your life. Suddenly, you are the underdog; you aren't as good, because you don't have the coveted thing or you're not the idolized person. Hmm... This sounds similar to a very old commandment. Something to consider...

This third kind of wishing creates an unconscious longing and resentment that eventually leads to a learned helplessness, because you haven't recognized the desire within yourself. It has been said that a wish is just a fantasy unless it has been written down and a date has been given to it. But even before that can happen, there first needs to be the awareness that you have unfulfilled wishes in your life. They might seem unrealistic given your current situation; however, they will provide clues as to how you really want to be living your life.

So what does all this mean? Wish. Wish lots. Be aware of your wishes, write them down in your Enlightened Wealth book, and then decide consciously if they are worth pursuing, modifying or

throwing away. When you've done that, decide what can be done, how and when to do it. Then seriously go after discovering how, who, what, where and all the other details that are necessary to make them reality. The awareness and the pursuit are where the best rewards are found.

Best wishes!

First Believe

Believe you can dream and that it can become real, and you will begin to create the vision for many areas of your life. What does vision have to do with success, financial or otherwise? EVERYTHING. Without a clear vision, life will easily sidetrack you. Opportunities will come and go and your daily decisions will be made more on your feelings at the time than on a long-term vision for your life.

How do you really see yourself living? Where do you see yourself living? How do you dress? What do you look like? Who are your friends? What do you drive? What do you do with your time? What is your money doing for others? How are you going to be remembered when you die?

If you think this isn't important, or that it sounds materialistic, or that it's okay to have a vague idea about what you want to do with your life, just try to actually do any serious financial planning without it. If you only have a hazy idea about the direction of your life, then how are you going to understand what sort of income is

required to support that lifestyle so you can begin to plan for it? If you believe strongly in particular causes, could you do more good with more money?

The vision must be crystal clear and must cover ALL areas of your life. When you have this, it will pull you through any challenges that life might throw your way (I'm speaking from experience here). It will guide your decision-making process. It will ensure that you are aware of opportunities and information and the people who can help you realize your vision.

Why am I passionate about this? This concept started me on my journey into learning about how people relate to money. I specialized in retirement planning and would ask clients over and over again to answer a few simple questions: When would they like to retire? How much income did they think they required in today's dollars to fund the lifestyle they envisioned living when they retired? The frustrating answer, most of the time, was, "Just tell me how much money I'm going to have and I'll figure it out from there." These were often the same people that would question their portfolio and my management if the returns didn't meet those of the illustrations we had done before making investments. They had taken themselves out of the position of control and had made it someone else's responsibility (in this case mine) to decide their lifestyle after they left work.

Stop for a minute and consider this issue as it relates to your whole life. If you only have a vague idea of what you would like to accomplish, how you would like to live your life and what you would like to do with your time, then who is in control? Are you living your life inside the "box" of your current income? Or are you consciously creating income opportunities to support your desired lifestyle? Or are you living a lifestyle that is paid for on credit?

You can feel guilty, critical or fearful of a debt lifestyle or you can choose to see this as your desire for a more expensive lifestyle. You can use this as an opportunity to take charge, get motivated and look beyond your current situation. You can also choose to see your debt as having provided you with some wonderful experiences that you would not have otherwise had. Either way, you become aware of your choices and choose to take charge of your future while still enjoying today. You can't go back and erase the debt, you can only go forward. Use your debt as an incentive to change and be grateful for the opportunities it has given you so far.

You are the only one who is responsible for your life. If you aren't taking charge of your choices, then someone else is. "If you don't know where you're going, you'll probably end up somewhere else!" said David Campbell, author of the book by that title. Someone else will tell you how much money you make, when you work and when you can take holidays. This means that someone else can tell you what sort of home you will live in, and where, what you will wear, what you will drive, who and what you can influence outside of yourself.

If you have a big vision for a grand lifestyle or to do big things in the world around you, are you settling for less? Or are you justifying your current position because you don't know how or because the distance between today's reality and tomorrow's possibilities is too far? You know, you don't get the beautiful view from the mountaintop from a single bound upwards. You climb one step at a time and maybe stop to rest, reassess and then rejoice at your progress so far. You can climb as much as you can, when you can, and enjoy the view along the way. If it's a big mountain you also don't get there without a plan, a map and perhaps a guide. All the details of your climb need to be documented—the same with your financial plans.

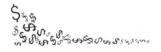

22

Vision. Goals. Purpose. These are the qualities that give your life direction. This doesn't mean that you are to become driven or that you are to set huge goals for yourself—absolutely not (unless you really want to). It means that you are to become aware of what is important to you and to live your life according to the vision you have for yourself and your family. It all comes back to awareness. Become aware of what inspires you and then project that into a vision for your future. It might be financial, or it might be a vision for your family, or your health or your contribution to your community. Then take control of your circumstances and your future to watch the miracles unfold.

If I didn't have a vision of myself as someone slim, energetic, healthy, confident, loving, fun, inspirational, friendly and financially successful, would I have created a daily habit to drink water first thing in the morning? Would I eat as many cucumbers as I do? Would I read the books I do? Would my choices of how I spend my time, who I spend my time with, and how I spend my/our money be different?

If I didn't have a crystal-clear vision for the type of home I'd like to live in with my family, the type of car I would like to drive, the garden I see around my home, its décor, the dinner parties, the pool parties, the kids playing, the things I like to do with my time, the way I like to dress, the kind of artwork I like, the colors that appeal to me, my ideal day, my ideal vacation, my ideal family life, my ideal relationship, and the influence I'd like to make in my community and around the world, do you think it might cause me to make different decisions throughout my day? I'm completely sure that I wouldn't set goals for how much money I want to give to charity each year. I would say different things to my husband and to my daughter. I would eat differently. I would

read different books. I would do different things and make different choices—period.

What is your vision? How do you envision your relationships, your family, your time, your home, your hobbies, your transportation, your ideal day, your health, your lifestyle and your legacy?

This isn't about being materialistic. This is about being aware of what inspires you, what is important to you, how you would like to live your life and what contribution you want to make to the world around you. Make decisions that are supportive of that vision, even if that vision is simply to stay the way you are today! Without vision, life will carry on. There will always be choices to make, and while each one will get you somewhere, you will deal with life's events as they come. However, speaking from personal experience again, without vision, when life throws a curve ball, it is too easy to get distracted, discouraged and passive about how you use your time.

Your crystal-clear vision is the necessary link to carry you from wherever you are today to wherever you want to go. Life isn't a dress rehearsal. We will arrive somewhere. We can either be a day older, a month older, a year older or ten years older or we can be all that and feel satisfied, fulfilled, happy and significant at the same time!

First believe you're worth it! Then create your vision and begin to make it real. It's your life. Live it on purpose!

BEGIN

Then Begin

"Until one is committed, there is hesitancy, the chance to draw back, always ineffectiveness, concerning all acts of initiative (and creation). There is one elementary truth, the ignorance of which kills countless ideas and splendid plans: that the moment one definitely commits oneself, then providence moves too. All sorts of things occur to help one that would never otherwise have occurred. A whole stream of events issues from the decision, raising in one's favour all manner of unforeseen incidents and meetings and material assistance which no man could have dreamed would have come his way."

W.H. Murray

Commitment. That's quite a word. It certainly has its implications and interpretations. Literally, it means "an act of committing to a charge or trust as; an agreement or pledge to do something in the future such as an engagement to assume a financial obligation at

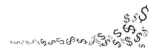

a future date, something pledged or the state of being obligated or emotionally impelled" (Merriam-Webster Online Dictionary).

Often, we hear people talk about commitment as though it is something they can avoid or something they are forced to do against their will. Perhaps we all need to realize we are always committed. We might not consciously be aware of our commitments, but the bottom line is that we are all committed to a particular outcome, either intentionally or unconsciously.

For example, I am writing this section late at night while having a midnight snack. Consciously, I am committed to getting the first draft completed. I am motivated and emotionally enthusiastic about that outcome. I am not obligated to do it tonight, but I made a conscious commitment to start this process so I am now conscious about following through on my intentions. If I feel forced into this outcome, it is because I purposely and consciously committed myself to this process. I could stop or change my mind, but I feel an obligation to my readers and to myself to continue.

Now, what else have I committed to by deciding to write this section tonight? My family is already asleep so I'm not sacrificing family time for writing time. I am probably committing myself to being tired tomorrow because I will not have a complete night's rest. Oh, well. Perhaps I am also unconsciously committing myself to being unhealthy because of my late night food choices. I will likely be tired tomorrow and I might be less inspired to get out the door to exercise. Interestingly, earlier in the evening, I made the commitment to stay up late in the first place when I accepted a cup of coffee after 8:00 pm.

Where we are today is a culmination of all our previous decisions, which ultimately, either consciously or unconsciously, lead us to

the place in our lives where I am writing this book and you are reading it. We are always committing ourselves to an outcome, either today or tomorrow. We may or may not be aware of those commitments, but consciously or unconsciously, they are still commitments.

If you consider the Webster's definition of commitment above, where a commitment is an agreement or a pledge to do something in the future, you need to stop and ask yourself, what exactly am I committed to, today and tomorrow? If you are committed to living today, are you also doing it with an eye to tomorrow? If you are committed to completing a task for tomorrow, are you doing it while also considering today?

Commitment obviously applies to many areas of life: health, relationships, finance. Since my area of expertise is in finance, let's consider some implications of commitment to financial success. You are committed to an outcome when you decide how you earn your money, how you spend your money, how and where you invest it, with whom you associate, what information you pursue, how you invest (or spend) your time and the list goes on and on.

When you complete the Enlightened Wealth section on goals and desires, you will easily see where some desires for something different in the future might begin to form. Awareness of desires is one thing, but it is an entirely different matter to make a conscious commitment to make decisions that are supportive of turning those desires into reality. If you desire anything different in your future than what you have today, then you will need to commit to creating that future rather than simply accepting today's circumstances as your only route.

Every decision and action is a commitment. It either supports a desired future vision, or it doesn't. If you have an awareness of something you would like in your life, such as more income, no debt, a bigger home, a nicer car, education for your children, a trip around the world, helping to end world hunger, more spare time and as many different desires as there are people to dream them up, then you need to consciously make decisions that will lead you in that direction. Otherwise, to know and not to do is not to know, and if that's the case, you really don't know where you want to be. You might wish you were somewhere else, had something else or did something else, but unless you act accordingly, you are not committed.

Commit

If you simply must have that $3.50 coffee and muffin snack, then be aware that you are making a commitment to enjoy that choice without reservation about whether or not it is good for you and whether or not it's too expensive. If you decide against spending money on disability insurance, then understand that you are committed to the outcome if you become sick or injured. If you have only one source of income, then understand that you are committed to accepting the risk associated with relying on that one income. If you buy the $400 TV set with the money from your savings account that was supposed to be for your holiday, then you have committed to watching someone else enjoy his or her holiday before you enjoy your own. If you use your credit card to purchase something on sale at 15 percent off because it was a good deal, even though you know you don't have the money at that moment, then know that you have really committed to paying more for that item in the long run. If you take on debt of any kind, you have committed your future income to paying for past pleasure.

This list can go on and on and can work in reverse just as easily. You make commitments by deciding not to do something, such as invest, pay bills on time or turn down the "good deal", just as easily as you do when you decide to do something. So, commit! Because, whether you like it or not, you already are.

On that note, I am committed to getting some sleep tonight so I can enjoy my day tomorrow as much as I have enjoyed writing this section, but I will leave you with a simple exercise to help you focus.

Complete the following sentence in a notebook, journal, or in the space provided in the Enlightened Wealth Journal available at www.MoneyMinding.com and know that you are taking an important first step toward beginning your new, committed journey.

> *I am committed to this process and to maintaining this book to the highest standards. I know I will achieve my goals because:*

When you are finished, sign and date your comments, then keep your notebook or journal handy and refer to your commitment often.

Ongoing Commitments

"If it's going to be, it's up to me to do the things that unsuccessful people don't want to do."

Tracy Piercy

Ongoing commitments are like goals, but they are more than that. They are decisions you make that will help you reach your goals. One example, from my own life, is a decision I made several years ago that I would have a glass of water first thing in the morning before I ate or drank anything else. I also made a commitment to maintain a banking transaction record (checkbook) of our personal accounts. I made another one to answer the review questions from Enlightened Wealth each night, at least in my head, before I went to sleep to keep my mind focused on where I was going and what I was doing daily to get there.

You can make a commitment to say, "I love you" every day to your spouse or to hug your children daily. You can decide that you will

open and pay your bills the minute they come. You can decide you will read from a positive book for a few minutes each day. There are as many possibilities as there are people reading this book.

You must first change your mind before you can change your life. Decide you are going to realize your life goals no matter what, then follow through with the necessary actions to make them a reality. It has been said that 80 percent of financial success is the way we think and that 20 percent is the "how-to." Your commitments along your Enlightened Wealth journey will become a key component. Why? Because, as you uncover information and implement small changes, you will begin thinking differently. When you think differently, you will develop your own ideas about what you would like to accomplish and how you intend to accomplish them. A one percent increase in productivity that is consistently carried out will yield far more than a one percent increase in results over time!

Some of the commitments you make will be to complete certain tasks, research certain concepts, and contact certain people and to participate in certain activities. Perhaps you are already doing all you can so the commitments you make to yourself might be in the area of consistency. You might even consider making commitments to important people in your life. Whatever your commitments, they are not ideas or "shoulds." They are commitments—things you have decided to do and will continue to do without excuse!

Be sure to refer back to this section to ensure that you are staying true to yourself. How sad, when you find it easy to keep your commitments to everyone else, yet don't respect yourself enough to keep your personal commitments. As I've said before, you are always committed to an outcome. Sometimes that commitment is made consciously, and at other times, it is made unconsciously because you haven't made a decision to take control of your future.

Where you are today is entirely due to your past commitments and decisions. Whether you realize it or not, you have been committed to your current situation and you are making commitments to your future with every decision you make. How about making a decision to at least be conscious of the future you are creating today?

Make your commitments. Write them on a page in your notebook or your journal and make them happen. Along the way, remember: if three friends are sitting on a bench, and one decides to move on, how many are left? Three. That's because deciding to do something and actually following through with action are completely separate issues. Decisions require action.

Have fun along the way. It's not about sacrifice and struggle. It's about fun, laughter and making a difference!

Your Expectations, Goals and Focus

As you continue your Enlightened Wealth journey, take some time to answer the following questions to begin to get clear on what you really expect for your future. There will be plenty of opportunity to revise your answers. This is not something to be researched and it is not a test. Rather, it is your process of gaining clarity. You are growing clear on your expectations and desired outcome throughout your journey.

DATE: _____

1. **What would I like to accomplish in this process?**

2. **Why is this important to me?**

3. **How do I see my life in one year? What are my one-year goals?**

4. **How do I see my life in five years? What are my five-year goals?**

5. How do I see my life in 10 years? What are my 10-year goals?

6. If I had died this afternoon, what would my obituary say (about my life, my accomplishments, my family, etc.)?

7. If I were 100 years old and were writing my obituary while I was sitting in my rocking chair, what would it say about my life? (Also, where would my rocking chair be?)

8. What area of my life do I feel I need to emphasize the most? (Some examples are health, family, finances, career, personal time, relationships, spirituality, creativity, etc.)

9. Why do I feel that way?

10. Are there any short-term or long-term consequences to not dealing with this area?

11. In considering life areas, can I rank in order of priority my top three primary areas of focus?

   • Career

   • Education

   • Health

   • Family

   • Spousal relationship

   • Relationship with children

   • Relationships with parents or other family members

   • Friends and social activities

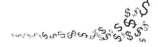

- **Hobbies and entertainment**
- **Spirituality**
- **Finances**
- **Community or volunteer involvement**
- **Home**
- **Other** _____
- **Other** _____
- **Other** _____

12. **Why did I select these top priorities?**

13. **Why are they important to me?**

14. **What, if any, are the consequences of not focusing on those areas of my life?**

15. **Does this worry me?**

Your Priorities

"A hundred years from now it will not matter what my bank account was, the sort of house I lived in, or the kind of car I drove... but the world may be different because I was important in the life of a child."

Author Unknown

This is my favorite saying and one that became significant at my mother's funeral. It is something we all need to take to heart.

Rarely is money ever our top priority. It is merely a cover to what is really important. We know this because if a child or a family member is sick and needs attention, how important does work become? When there is a family or personal crisis, very few people continue to put work as their number one priority.

It is easy to be fooled into thinking that money is the most important priority because it will allow you to have the things that society says are important to have. Often you end up putting "making a living" ahead of other areas in life because you feel a sense of responsibility and obligation to provide for food, shelter, clothing, cars, holidays, activities, etc. However, if you are making a living to provide for your family, yet you end up spending more time with your co-workers than with your families, you create conflict within yourself. There is a happy medium somewhere that is different for everyone. You can easily fool yourself into thinking that you are doing the best for your children by working hard to excel at your job, putting in overtime, taking extra courses, bringing work home—often for no extra money because you work on a fixed salary. Yet, most of the time what your children really desire is quality time with their parents and quality time does not come without quantity time.

Other priorities that often get overlooked are personal health, personal development and spiritual life. How often do you hear people say they "don't have time to exercise" or "don't have time to eat a healthy meal" or "don't have time to go to the bathroom"? Well, the strategy of working hard day and night might work for some people some of the time. However, if you lose your health, how effective will you be at work or at providing for your family?

Achieving financial independence is not something to be attained "at all costs." There is no end result, just "a progressive realization of a worthwhile dream"—a dream that encompasses the most important areas of your life.

What's interesting is what we do when something happens to a family member, friend or to ourselves. If you get sick, are you really rushing off to meetings and putting in the same amount of overtime? If your child gets sick or needs attention, do you continue to put in the same effort at work? Can you even concentrate at all? I could still continue to work after our financial

loss, but when my mother died, I barely made it through the day for months. When my husband injured himself recently and was taken to the hospital by ambulance, then had surgery a day later—did I continue to work? Did I sleep? Did I eat?

On an even bigger scale, when there is a disaster somewhere in the world, are you glued to the news? Do you jump into action to help out in some way?

Events like these provide clues into our life priorities. Ask yourself the following questions to help uncover your true priorities and their importance to you.

DATE: _____

1. **What is most important to me in my life today? Why? How will I remember this when I am thinking or doing anything of financial consequence?**

2. **How much of my day is dedicated to my top life priority? Why? How will I remember this when I am thinking or doing anything of financial consequence?**

3. **Is what I'm doing most taking me closer to my top priority? Why? How will I remember this when I am thinking or doing anything of financial consequence?**

4. **What can I do immediately to move me in the direction of my life's focus? Why? How will I remember this when I am thinking or doing anything of financial consequence?**

5. How will my life be different if I commit now to focus on my highest priority? Why? How will I remember this when I am thinking or doing anything of financial consequence?

6. With who, where, with what and how can I get help to stay focused on what is truly important?

Your Blessings

Perhaps you have completed goal-setting exercises before. Perhaps you are a diligent goal-setter. Or perhaps you have never set goals and the questions on expectations, goals and focus were completely foreign and scary to you. Regardless of past experience with goals, you will find that as you clarify your vision, there is likely to be resistance if you find a gap between your current and your ideal situation. The natural first reaction is to feel lack, guilt, and remorse or fear that if you allow yourself to dream and to set goals, you might not be able to attain them. If you dwell in fear, the shortcomings will become your focus and this certainly isn't conducive to making positive changes in your life.

Along life's journey, there are a few principles, actually, rules that are necessary to accomplish anything of value, whether they are a financial change or a personal change. If you are not grateful for all that you have today, there will never be any satisfaction for any future acquisitions or changes to your life. Just take a look around. Where you are today might not be where you had hoped to be or where you had expected to be. If you have any sort of vision for

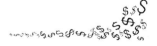

the future, your current reality might be a long way from your vision, but where you are is exactly where you are meant to be right now—even if it's not really where you thought you "should" be or wanted to be.

This section of your Enlightened Wealth journey is designed to help you work through any fears and feelings of lack. It is also meant to help you set and reach for significant goals.

Starting with a blank page in your notebook or journal, you will make a list of all the blessings and good things you have in your life today. Record anything you are grateful for—ANYTHING! These could be simple, such as "I like my smile" or more abstract things like "I've learned a lot of lessons." They can also be concrete such as the money you have in the bank, your job, your family, etc.

How long should the list be? The longer, the better. It makes sense to me that if you have many desires, you would want to balance that list with blessings. So, in financial terms, if your blessings are your assets and your desires are your liabilities (only because they haven't manifested into your reality yet), then you need to balance your list. The list of desires is just ahead in your book, but I will give you a heads-up that your instructions are to complete a list of 101 desires. Therefore, you need to come up with 101 blessings on your balance sheet. (See "Your Desires" for more information.)

Your list of blessings can include anything from the past, present or future. When I first published this exercise, people commented about their experiences, which were very similar to my own. We found that, at first, it seemed like a daunting task or, at least, that it was more challenging to come up with 101 blessings than it would be to make the list of desires. In reality, however, the blessings

flowed onto the paper much quicker and more easily than in the exercise to come up with the 101 desires.

If you don't have the time to reflect and to be grateful for what you have and where you are and to make a record of your blessings, then you also won't have time to do the rest of the activities in your Enlightened Wealth book. Gratitude for, and awareness of, all you have are the foundations for growth and change and the first principle written in most books on success.

Without gratitude and awareness of your blessings, there can be no further change; anything further just simply won't be recognized. You will always be searching and never finding. Life is in all the small wonders, the little blessings that happen along the journey.

What can you learn from this exercise? Quite simply: There is power in awareness. You really do have a lot to be grateful for— you just have to stop and become aware of all that you do have. It is not new that a grateful heart is a happy heart. As with your list of desires in the upcoming section, it isn't something to do once and then move on; it is something to refer to again and again. Enjoy the process and may your blessings be plenty! Have fun! Let me know how you make out! Send a message to info@MoneyMinding.com. I'm sure you will discover you are richer than you think.

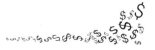

Your Personal, Non-Financial Assets and Resources

> *"Your presence is a present to the world,*
> *Count your blessings, not your troubles,*
> *And within you are so many answers."*
>
> **Excerpt from Collin McCarty's**
> *Things to Always Remember*

In business, this category would be called goodwill. In our personal lives, we have assets such as education, experience and personal contacts that are most often completely overlooked, underrated or forgotten. Some of these items might be from your list of 101 blessings; some will be new.

If you are planning a life change, such as a move or a new career, this section will be particularly useful. The purpose is to awaken you to the reality that you are worth so much more than the dollars and cents demonstrated by your financial assets. You already have

so much to be grateful for and much abundance in your life that is easy to overlook because it is easier to focus on the negative, the lack and the gap that exists between your current reality and the one you dream of.

The following exercise will also help stimulate you to think about the abundance in your life and the variety of options available to you. Start by making a list of the assets or resources you have in your life, then for each item answer the following questions:

1. **Reason why this in an asset or resource.**

2. **How might I use this to my advantage?**

3. **What might I offer in exchange?**

You can be creative and brainstorm many ideas for each asset you come up with. Have fun brainstorming all your contacts, resources, ideas and experiences that have value—even if they don't have a price tag on them today. You are worth so much more than the cash in your bank account.

The question regarding what you might offer in exchange is designed to help you develop your giving attitude. Whenever you give with sincerity and without expectation, you demonstrate abundance and prepare yourself to receive all that you desire. The purpose here is to help you think in terms of giving as well as getting and to stimulate creative ways you might trade resources to provide mutual benefit to you and someone else. For example, if you have a knowledge or a skill set and require some referrals to assist in a career change, you could offer your services to the people you are asking for help. Again, be creative and have fun with it! You never know what doors will be opened to you along the way.

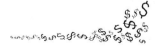

Your Vision of Personal Financial Success

Financial success is a feeling you get when you have enough money to be, do and have all that you desire. It's the feeling that money can buy, not the stuff itself. Only you will know the feeling financial success will bring you. Only you will be able to determine what it will take to create that feeling. When you can identify with the underlying emotion you are trying to accomplish with financial success, you will have an easier time enjoying your current situation and your journey towards your financial goals. You will be able to find ways to create the emotions even before the actual dollar amount has been realized. When you understand the emotion you are after, then you can consider what amount of money in a lump sum or in a regular cash flow is required to maintain the feeling. Examples might be a feeling of relief, relaxation, contribution, satisfaction or pride. Whatever the feeling is, it is an important step toward the realization of financial independence.

True, you don't need money to be happy, but you have more choices with it than without. Maybe financial success is more about something that it is not, such as stress, doing without, worry, restriction. Maybe it's more time to do the things that are important to you such as being with family and friends, volunteering for community causes, learning, being with yourself or any activity you can imagine that currently receives less time than you would like.

Maybe financial success feels like just where you currently are, but you're not sure if you can maintain the lifestyle or if you are doing all you can with what you have because you have questions that are unanswered. What do you do with this? Understand what it will feel like to have the confidence that you are in control. Start with an attitude of gratitude and expect that you will reach your goals and that you are doing all you can with what you have.

Somewhere along the way, you have designed rules around what it means to be successful. You will have a very personal opinion of what success looks like in terms of material possessions and activities and the sort of person who has acquired these attributes. These ideas might be positive, but they could be negative. Understanding that you have certain rules around financial success is an important distinction to make. The rules and ideas you have are your very own individual rules; no one else has the same ones.

You can set yourself up to succeed or fail, depending on the rigidity of the rules you create around what it takes to be financially successful. For example, if you have designed a rule that says in order to be successful financially, you must have $10,000,000 cash, make more than $1,000,000 a year, live in a certain neighborhood, drive the best cars and entertain at the most elite establishments, then you will not accept any level of success

outside of these rules. This would make it difficult to enjoy your journey and to be grateful for your current situation.

Money in the hands of good people can do good things. Money is neither good nor bad. It just is. It's not bad to have money. There is nothing wrong with having it. Since success doesn't normally mean going without, you need to consider the important judgments, values and influences that affect your overall financial satisfaction.

You already have some degree of financial success. You just need to be able to recognize it first—beginning with developing that attitude of gratitude for what you already have. If you can understand what you have already accomplished, you will begin to believe that perhaps you have already experienced what financial success feels like to you and therefore will be capable of creating it again. Your review of your list of blessings and non-financial assets and your feelings toward those lists is an important consideration in your financial journey. Regardless of where you are compared to where you would like to be, you are already successful. Learning to recognize these feelings will help you to identify with the real reasons for your enlightened wealth journey.

An important exercise in learning to recognize your personal view of financial success is to define it in your own words, in an emotionally compelling way that means something to you. The questions that follow will help you get clear (remember to sign and date your answer):

1. What does financial success mean to me?

2. When I've accomplished my personal level of financial success, how will I feel?

3. When I've accomplished my personal level of financial success, how will I imagine myself as being?

    a. And doing?

    b. And enjoying?

    c. And having?

4. When I've accomplished my personal level of financial success, how will I see myself?

Your Why

"The size of your success is measured by the strength of your desire, the size of your dream and how you handle disappointment along the way."

Author Unkown

This is really quite a personal question and the answers will be different even between spouses. Understanding why you haven't achieved your financial vision and the consequences of not doing so are an extension of the physical goal. Why is this so important to understand? Because if you don't have a compelling reason to do something, the time and effort required to do the planning, reviewing and research for your Enlightened Wealth journey will become just that: a time-consuming effort.

Goal provide you with direction and tell you that where you are is not where you want to be. Setting goals is the starting place

to taking action. The reasons for setting goals (and achieving them) are actually far more important. When you have a strong enough reason to do something, the way to achieve the goal will find its way to you.

In the exercise that follows, there is a component to the questions where you will be asked to record the reasons you want something. This will help you find simple pleasures such as "feel more relaxed, have more time with family and have more fun." There is also a "Why" component to help you search for all the important reasons you would want the items listed as reasons. For example, if one of your reasons was to "feel more relaxed," your reasons why might be, "better health, more fun to be around, better relationship with spouse and family, have more fun, enjoy life, have energy to do other things, etc." You will inevitably experience lots of overlap, and you will have many why's for each reason. Take advantage of the bank pages in your notebook or journal to record your thoughts as well as the specifics as you write your goals and reasons.

Having compelling reasons to do something is the first half of the equation. The other half is the consequence of not realizing your goals. Sometimes fear is the motivation that ultimately becomes the driving force. Imagine how much effort you could put into holding on to your money compared to the effort you put into making it. Once you have accumulated money, you will go to great effort to make sure you don't lose any of it because you don't want to face the consequences. Fear is also the same reason why many people in their mid-forties or early fifties suddenly become very concerned with retirement planning. The reality of their age sets in and finally registers in their mind that they are getting close to that golden age. If they have any chance of leaving the workforce, they need to be highly motivated to take control of their financial decisions.

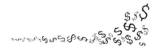

When you complete this section of your Enlightened Wealth journey, you will have a tool to help you realize that there are compelling reasons to pay attention to your finances and that there are consequences of not following through on your commitments to yourself. If you can complete this section honestly and without inserting any "shoulds" into the table, you will give yourself more power toward achieving your goal of financial independence—whatever that might be for you.

When society says you "should" have so much money saved by a particular age, you "should" retire at a particular age, you "should" drive a certain type of car, you "should" live in a particular neighborhood and you "should" dress a certain way, there is no strong personal motivation to work towards these goals. You need to know why you would personally desire something different in your life before you will act on it. From this framework, you will develop ownership and control over your financial destiny.

1. **Start by creating a list of reasons why you want financial success.**

2. **For each reason, find a reason why this is important to you.**

3. **For each item, list the consequences of not succeeding.**

4. **Finally, for each item, write why the consequence worries you.**

Your Desires

Sometimes setting goals and looking at priorities is a new and different idea for some people. Even if you have been setting goals for years, they can sometimes seem like intellectual exercises rather than passionate driving forces directing your behavior.

Now that you know where you are starting from and why you want anything different, it's easier to see how your current situation will become the catalyst to helping you realize your desires. Your desires will continuously inspire you while you journey toward your goals. The idea is to create a long list of specific things that you would like to accomplish or realize in your life. Your list will contain things, activities and feelings, people you hope to meet, places you hope to go, things you plan to accomplish and anything else that comes to your mind. It can be as simple as buying a new pair of shoes or as complex as owning a resort in the Caribbean or building an orphanage in Africa. Your items are your list so simple things like a hot coffee in the morning already made for you when you wake up is as appropriate to write as appearing on national television for some terrific deed you did.

The process of creating the list will be something like writing a Christmas wish list when you were a kid. Updating it will give you some inspiration that: (a) there are things in life that you would like, which will help you overcome boredom and stagnation and help you continue to move forward; and (b) you really are moving forward because you will visibly see the items that you have crossed off your list as they become real. Your list will constantly evolve. Play with it. You will be surprised at what you are able to think into existence once you have committed it to paper.

Do you remember the saying, "Watch your thoughts; they become words. Watch your words; they become actions. Watch your actions; they become habits. Watch your habits; they become character. Watch your character; it becomes your destiny"?

Awareness is vital to your enjoyment of life and to fulfilling your life's purpose. With that in mind, sometimes we aren't even aware of our true desires. What do you really wish for? Why? What will it mean to your life if this is present today? What will it mean to your life if this is never present?

Beginning on a blank page, make your list of 101 things to be, do, have, see, share or experience in your life. The key to this list is the number of items. Don't stop until you have 101. Have fun with your list—it shouldn't feel like work. The easy, top-of-mind items come first, but the more important things start to come to mind as you keep going. When you're done, share the process and your experiences with someone you know. If you have a spouse, you can each make a separate list and then compare notes. It will make a fabulous and unique "date night."

The process of writing your desires and developing the clarity of purpose needed to complete the list of 101 items will help you

recognize desires beyond the material things on the surface of your day-to-day life. Also, the process of writing the desires gives them life, which means you will have a 95 percent greater likelihood of realizing them than if you just thought about them. It has been scientifically proven that written goals will bring you closer to realizing them, and you have already proven it yourself if you have ever tried to go grocery shopping without a list.

When your list is complete, you will want to review the items and set some time frames for realization. You can categorize according to your lifetime: 20 years, 10 years, five years, three years, one year or whatever time frame works for you. Do your desired items correspond to the goals you wrote in the "Expectations, Goals and Focus" section of this book? As you set goals in the future, you will have your lists with you so the process is dynamic, yet always takes you one step closer to your ideal reality. (See "Your Goals" next for more information.)

When you have completed your list and a time frame analysis (described next), there are also some simple and fun exercises you can do on your own to help you begin to connect it to your personal view of success and your "why." Whole books have been written on the concepts, so I will simply state the activity and why it is important to practice.

The first activity is to make seeing, touching, feeling and smelling your ideal lifestyle a regular activity. This means that, at least monthly, you can go places, such as touring new homes, travel agencies, car dealers, country clubs, motor home dealers, marinas, etc. You can research different restaurants, different charities, different businesses and different activities of other people in different economic circumstances. You need to do whatever is

necessary so that you can actually experience what your ideal
future will be like.

The second activity is to begin to create a scrapbook, file folder
or, my personal favorite, a photo album of your future. My
photo album is a single, photo-sized, mini-album, which holds
approximately 30 pictures. Its pages are filled with images, sayings,
goals and thoughts about my future rather than about my past. I
look at this book all the time! This might seem too simple and
unimportant, yet it may be the most important exercise you can do
to realize the level of financial success you desire.

When you reinforce your written goals with visuals you are
constantly reinforcing them, which is a vital exercise in realizing
where you are going and why you're going there.

Make your list of 101 things to be, do, have, see, share and
experience over your lifetime. Then look at those 101 items and
know that each day there is always something to look forward to.
These are concrete, material items that, as they come into fruition,
you may cross off your list and replace with something new.
This way, you can track your progress as your list evolves along
your life's journey.

BECOME

Your Goals

Goals direct your life. However, sometimes they seem to be in conflict with each other. In the "Priorities" section of Enlightened Wealth, it is easy to say that being in the best physical shape and to excelling at work are priorities. Yet, in reality, juggling the time and focus to reach all your goals is challenging. That is why looking at your priorities when setting goals is absolutely essential. They will direct you to rank your goals according to your true priorities.

You will have goals in various areas of your life that are not financially related. Just because this program is about personal finance, does not mean that all of your goals are going to be financial. There are different areas of your life where you will set goals. One area is life priorities, such as health, family, spirituality and career. Another is life focus, such as what you do with your free time, personal development, financial independence, more money, etc. Another area is specific to the world of finance: paying down debt, saving for a specific goal, preserving your estate, controlling cash flow, etc. The challenge is to balance all three and to keep them all in focus as you prepare your financial plans and

go about your daily activities. This is work that financial and life coaches do: help to keep the focus, the balance and implement the systems and programs to bring your goals into reality.

After completing your lists of priorities, blessings, non-financial assets and desires, you will be building a vision for your life and developing some ideas about what you already have available to help you bridge from where you are to where you're going. You will be getting clear on some lifetime achievement you're aiming for or answers to questions such as what you want for your life, who you want to become, how you want to be remembered and what legacy you would like to leave. When you consider why you would like to realize a particular desire, the reason for it will also help you establish a specific goal to accomplish within a particular time frame.

So, what do you do with these lists? The answer is to review your list of desires and decide whether each item is something to be realized in one of the categories below. When you have decided, put a number beside the item that corresponds to the appropriate category:

Over your lifetime.

Within ten years.

Within five years.

Within three years.

Within one year.

Then review your list again and record your top one-year goals on a fresh page or card you can keep with you. You might want to consider the MoneyMinding® Priority cards which also have some spending reminder questions on them to keep you aware of your goals as you use your cash. Having your written goals in plain site and particularly at your point of contact with your money will move you toward reaching your one-year goals easier and faster. The Priority cards and spending questions can be reproduced from the back of this book.

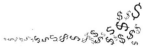

Your Ongoing Desires

"If one advances confidently in the direction of his dreams, and endeavors to live the life which he has imagined, he will meet with a success unexpected in common hours."
Henry David Thoreau

What is the difference between ongoing desires and goals? Ongoing desires are specific qualities of life or activities, such as having loving relationships, vibrant health, great friends, peace of mind and a calm attitude. Goals, on the other hand, are specific, measurable items that can be realized with certainty. Ongoing desires involve attitudes and character traits, but are different from ongoing commitments in that they really are subjective and only measurable by you. They are reminders of qualities of life and actions and activities that will take you toward your lifetime achievements with ease and grace. They will add to your fun and enjoyment along your journey.

To begin to identify your ongoing desires, start another list and answer the following items for each of the items you identify:

1. **What is the specific desire or quality of life you would like to experience?**

2. **What is the reason this is a desire?**

3. **How will you know if you're successful?**

And, what is the importance on a scale of 1 – 5 (1 low and 5 high) for each desire listed. The category called, "How you will know if you are successful" has the purpose to help you provide a unit of measurement for some of these intangible or subjective items such as to become a public speaker, or to learn to play the piano, or to have a great relationship with your kids. These are some of my personal lifetime desires. I particularly need to clarify the public speaking desire because, technically, I have been speaking publicly for most of my career, so I need to recognize that I need to clearly define what being a public speaker is to me. The same goes for playing the piano. Today, I can actually play "Mary Had a Little Lamb," but my lifetime desire has a significantly higher standard than that. I seem, also, to have a great relationship with my daughter, but I really haven't got another reference point since I only have the one child and have never been a mother before.

At this point in my life, increasing my piano-playing skills is not one of my top priorities. I have it written down on my list of 101 desires, and it's important enough that I have also listed it in my "ongoing desires" list as a more general note so that I can participate in playing beautiful piano music. I review this list of ongoing desires, along with my list of 101 items, to help me stay

focused and to set my shorter-term goals. I recognize that because playing the piano more proficiently is one of my lifetime dreams, I will tinker away whenever I have an opportunity and participate with my daughter as she takes lessons. This way, I get to work toward two of my ongoing desires and lifetime desires. As I've said before, "If you don't know where you're going and why, you'll probably end up somewhere else!" Goals, priorities and ongoing desires are all tools to help guide your journey.

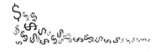

Your Daily Review

"You have been given this day to use as you will. You can waste it or use it for good. What you do today is important because you are exchanging a day of your life for it. When tomorrow comes, this day will be gone forever; in its place is something that you have left behind...let it be something good."

Author Unknown

The only real obstacle in any situation is in your mind. It's not what happens to you that is important, but how you react and interpret the event. You can choose to focus on all the things you didn't do, or on the things that went wrong, or on the things that aren't happening, or that don't exist in your life; or you can focus on all that is good. When you choose to see the blessings in your life, you are actually creating more of all that is good. You are more peaceful, more loving and more grateful. If you do not learn to appreciate each day and all that it brings, you will not recognize the positive changes you are creating. Life is not about what you have, what you do or any material possessions. It is about living daily and enjoying each moment for what it is—nothing more, nothing less.

As you journey toward the realization of your own personal financial goals, you will notice there are many small and simple changes that can be implemented into your daily routine to simplify the process. None will be as powerful as training your mind to recognize and enjoy day-to-day living and to anticipate the rewards of your efforts.

Asking yourself some simple questions before you go to bed each night will help you put a peaceful end to your day. By learning to ask good questions and to recognize the positive in every situation, you will succeed at whatever you set out to do and you will enjoy whatever comes your way. I encourage you to answer these Enlightened Wealth MoneyMinding® review questions on paper so that you affirm the importance of the events. I usually use one or two words only to answer my questions, and then, if there is something more detailed that I'd like to remember, I record that separately.

The questions that follow are designed for short, simple answers. If it feels as though you are always writing the same answer, good! That is where the power comes from. If you are always rewarded with a smile from a particular person in your life, and you are always grateful for the same people or experiences, then continuously writing these feelings will reinforce the attitude and help you to enjoy more of the same.

Likewise, if you find that whatever you could do better is always the same, then you have a terrific place to start to improve. It will also help you to get clear on why you might be feeling as though

you're struggling or seeming to come up with the same results day after day, week after week, month after month. Life was not meant to be a struggle, so enjoy this process and understand that the only real obstacles to your success are your own thoughts. Therefore, take the time and make the effort to do the exercise daily. It will become a ritual you look forward to and can share with others in your life. You will be rewarded in ways you never knew. You will also discover you already have a richer and more abundant life than you first thought and that you have all the resources you need to move forward toward your life's dreams—because, "As I think, so I become."

The Daily Review Questions

1. **What was I grateful for?**
   my home

2. **What made me smile?**
   watching kids play

3. **What could I do better?**
   exercise

4. **What were my challenges?**
   getting up early

5. **What was the best of today?**
   afternoon tea and book

6. **What did I give or share?**
   encouragement and inspiration

7. **What am I looking forward to?**
   client meeting

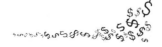

Become

This is the part of Enlightened Wealth where you get to go "hmmm"?

After 30 or 31 days of recording your short answers to the daily review questions in your notebook or journal take a moment to reflect on the themes, trends, consistencies and irregularities of your answers. Is there anything that needs additional focus? Is there anything that needs to be changed? If so, how and when? Use this opportunity to record your insights and to set your next short-term, 30-day goals.

Every 30 days, review your daily question answers, your goals, your commitments, your ongoing commitments and desires from your Enlightened Wealth journey. Make sure you record your new goals after doing your 'become' review and keep them where you can see them throughout the day.

1. **What was I grateful for the most? What can I do to recognize and to show appreciation for the gratitude I feel?**

2. What made me smile the most? What can I do to honor this in my life and to encourage these smiles more?

3. What can I do better? What steps can I take to acknowledge my feelings of wanting to improve that will help move me toward my ideal?

4. What were my biggest challenges? Who, what, when, where, and how can I move towards minimizing these challenges?

5. What was the best part of my day? What can I do to encourage more of these experiences?

6. What did I share most? How does this make me feel? Can I share more? Is it too much? Who benefited?

7. What am I looking forward to? Am I looking forward to the same experiences that contributed to the best part of my day, that made me smile, that made me feel grateful? Or is there a gap? What can I do to experience more of the experience I am looking forward to while acknowledging my other important daily experiences?

CONTINUE

Stay Focused

Congratulations and a huge acknowledgement to you for following through with the Enlightened Wealth exercises. Now, continue the habit, the momentum, and the wonderful experiences by recording the insights and priorities you are committed to going forward because the road to wealth is not something you graduate from. You begin and keep on becoming. At each step forward, you reflect and reset your goals and re-evaluate your priorities.

DATE: _____

1. **What is most important to me in my life today? Why? How will I remember this when I am thinking or doing anything of financial consequence?**

2. **How much of my day is dedicated to my top life priority? Why? How will I remember this when I am thinking or doing anything of financial consequence?**

3. Is what I am doing most taking me closer to my top priority? Why? How will I remember this when I am thinking or doing anything of financial consequence?

4. What can I do immediately to move me in the direction of my life's focus? Why? How will I remember this when I am thinking or doing anything of financial consequence?

5. How will my life be different if I commit now to focus on my highest priority? Why? How will I remember this when I am thinking or doing anything of financial consequence?

6. With who, where, with what, and how can I get help to stay focused on what's truly important?

Your Next Step

Your Enlightened Wealth journey is just that: it is the beginning. It is also the middle and the foundation of your lifelong financial journey.

Register at www.MoneyMinding.com to receive your free 12 Simple Steps Report which outlines the entire MoneyMinding® Makeover Program.

Share your lessons. Invite others to participate in taking control of their financial lives, to gain better understanding, to get better results, to set and reach spectacular goals, to make a significant positive impact in their lives and the lives of others. Together, we can make a difference!

Abundant blessings always,

Tracy

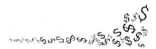

The MoneyMinding® Revolving Steps to Financial Independence

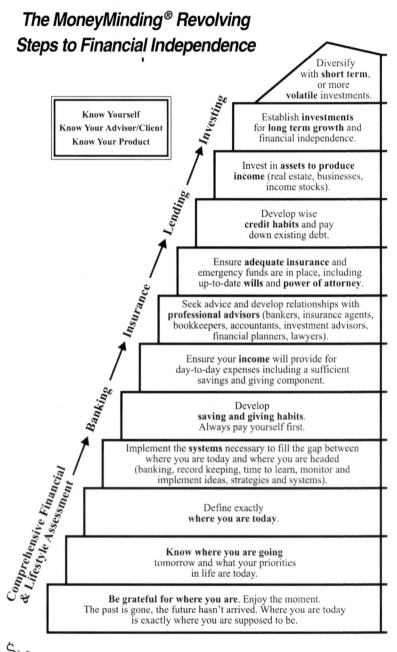

Know Yourself
Know Your Advisor/Client
Know Your Product

Investing

Lending

Insurance

Banking

Comprehensive Financial
& Lifestyle Assessment

Diversify with **short term**, or more **volatile** investments.

Establish **investments** for **long term growth** and financial independence.

Invest in **assets to produce income** (real estate, businesses, income stocks).

Develop wise **credit habits** and pay down existing debt.

Ensure **adequate insurance** and emergency funds are in place, including up-to-date **wills** and **power of attorney**.

Seek advice and develop relationships with **professional advisors** (bankers, insurance agents, bookkeepers, accountants, investment advisors, financial planners, lawyers).

Ensure your **income** will provide for day-to-day expenses including a sufficient savings and giving component.

Develop **saving and giving habits**. Always pay yourself first.

Implement the **systems** necessary to fill the gap between where you are today and where you are headed (banking, record keeping, time to learn, monitor and implement ideas, strategies and systems).

Define exactly **where you are today**.

Know where you are going tomorrow and what your priorities in life are today.

Be grateful for where you are. Enjoy the moment. The past is gone, the future hasn't arrived. Where you are today is exactly where you are supposed to be.

Asset Management
Credit Management
Risk Management & Legacy Planning
Cash Flow Management & Tax Planning
Personal Goals & Values

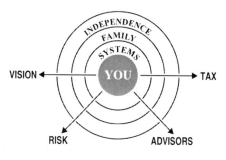

Notes

Priorities

$ _____

_____

_____

www.MoneyMinding.com

Priorities

$ _____

_____

_____

www.MoneyMinding.com

Priorities

$ _____

_____

_____

www.MoneyMinding.com

1. Why do I really want this now?
2. Do I have cash for it today?
3. How many hours, days, or weeks will I have to work to pay for this?
4. Is there something I need more?
5. Do I need to get rid of, or change anything before I buy this?
6. What if I don't buy it today? Can it wait?
7. Can I get by without it?

1. Why do I really want this now?
2. Do I have cash for it today?
3. How many hours, days, or weeks will I have to work to pay for this?
4. Is there something I need more?
5. Do I need to get rid of, or change anything before I buy this?
6. What if I don't buy it today? Can it wait?
7. Can I get by without it?

1. Why do I really want this now?
2. Do I have cash for it today?
3. How many hours, days, or weeks will I have to work to pay for this?
4. Is there something I need more?
5. Do I need to get rid of, or change anything before I buy this?
6. What if I don't buy it today? Can it wait?
7. Can I get by without it?

About Tracy Piercy

Tracy Piercy is a Certified Financial Planner (CFP) who goes beyond the parameters of traditional financial planning to integrate proven success principles with practical financial planning strategies. She has worked in the financial industry, in insurance, banking and as a top producing investment advisor with CIBC Wood Gundy for more than 15 years. Tracy has provided consulting and training to the industry, working closely with industry regulators, financial institutions and individual advisors. She has taught industry-required courses as well as developed programs for public education. She has trained with leaders in personal development and success, and personally experienced financial success and financial loss.

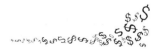

Tracy realized, through her client work as a successful investment advisor, that financial success was more than simply the right numbers, charts and technical information. Today, Tracy is the President of MoneyMinding® Inc., a company she founded. It is committed to financial education that includes the psychology of money and is focused on the individual as well as the technical understanding of financial strategies. She speaks, writes and develops tools to help both advisors and clients get better results. Her MoneyMinding® materials support the belief that regardless of your current economic situation, there are universal principles, strategies and techniques that aren't about sacrifice or frustration. Rather, they are about creating solutions for individual possibilities.

Tracy donates a percentage of all her earnings to charitable causes and is an advocate of philanthropic activities as well as delivering empowering messages that encourage individual success. Tracy has a wonderful husband of 10-plus years, and together they live in scenic Victoria, British Columbia, Canada with their beautiful daughter and small dog. They live in a century-old home, surrounded by great friends and family.

Notes

_____

_____

_____

_____

_____

_____

_____

_____

_____

_____

_____

_____

_____

_____

_____

_____

_____

_____

_____

_____

_____

_____

_____

_____

_____

_____

_____

Notes

_____

_____

_____

_____

_____

_____

_____

_____

_____

_____

_____

_____

_____

_____

_____

_____

_____

_____

_____

_____

_____

_____

_____

Notes

_____

_____

_____

_____

_____

_____

_____

_____

_____

_____

_____

_____

_____

_____

_____

_____

_____

_____

_____

_____

_____

_____

_____

_____

_____

_____